CW00486677

The Mediterranean Lifestyle:

Delicious Kitchen Recipes for Healthy Living Eating Well & Feeling Good Every day!

Jasmin Walters

Copyright © 2020 Jasmin Walters
All rights reserved.
ISBN: 9798692796967

CONTENTS

BOOK DESCRIPTION

I love the taste of a breakfast casserole with sausage and cheese exploding inside of my mouth and inducing a dopamine rush. Don't know what I'm talking about? Then it may very well be that the doctors prohibited you from eating all the tasty foods on account of your deteriorating health. But what if I were to tell you about a diet that is delicious and healthy at the same time? Introducing the Mediterranean diet is based on a dietary pyramid, which includes vegetables, legumes, fruits, nuts, beans, grains, unsaturated fats like olive oil and fish, among others.

Showcasing a large number of recipes like blackberry ginger overnight bulgur and bananas foster French toast, the names of which are enough to get your mouth watering, are now at your disposal to ensure that your health and taste buds go hand in hand. The Mediterranean lifestyle is versatile and has the potential to enrich one's life extravagantly.

What you will learn by reading this book:

- The workings of a Mediterranean lifestyle
- The numerous health benefits of the Mediterranean diet
- The secrets to weight loss without even trying
- Seasoned recipes based on the diet
- Traditional eating habits
- The flaws in your current lifestyle
- Better cooking methods

And so much more!

INTRODUCTION

The Mediterranean lifestyle is most famously known for inducing a sweet disposition, being closer to nature, and above all following the Mediterranean diet. As we grow older, most of our health problems can be traced back to an unhealthy diet.

The obscene amount of fats we consume and over the counter sugar and carbohydrates surely makes for early retirement. That said, we can now ponder over the alternatives. These certain foods have the capability to satisfy our appetites and assist us in our daily endeavors in today's fast-paced lifestyle. That's where the Mediterranean lifestyle factors in.

Most of us are under the illusion that switching our dietary habits is a challenging task, especially when you're on the periphery of your late-thirties and early-forties, and near impossible when you move into your fifties because your usual dietary habits have already been cemented and while it is possible to change them, we choose to invest our faith in doctors and medicines alike. So, let's talk some more about this diet before the doctor scrubs all of your favorite meals off the list.

CHAPTER1: WHAT IS THE MEDITERRANEAN DIET?

The Mediterranean diet is an eating the whole 30 approach that focuses more on whole foods. It's versatile in the sense that it's a mixture of traditional lifestyle habits of the people living in the areas that border the Mediterranean Sea, such as Greece, Italy, France, Spain, Morocco, and the like (Now you know where the name comes from).

The food pyramid is mainly structured on vegetables, legumes, fruits, nuts, beans, grains, unsaturated fats like olive oil and fish, among others. What's more? It even recommends a moderate amount of red wine to keep your taste buds on edge for whatever you consume next, whether it's a spiced chickpea with a green salad or a healthy breakfast of oatmeal with fruits and nuts. The diet focuses on the intake of natural foods as compared to over the counter processed foods to ensure a longer life span with fewer health complications.

Definition of the term:

As you already know, the dietary habits of people greatly vary from country to country and region to region. You may think that dietary habits basically encapsulate consuming whatever the person likes, but in reality, they are influenced by a number of factors such as traditional and cultural values.

Recipes are even passed down from generation to generation so that the food of the ancestors is distributed around the neighborhoods in every era. As millennials, we have grown accustomed to frozen foods because they are easy to defrost, easy to fry, and delicious to eat, but nobody will ever tell you how unhealthy they are until enough cholesterol is deposited in your vessels.

So maybe, it's time to take a detour to the French republic to cross-examine the dietary habits of the nation whose citizens have immaculate taste in almost everything. From there, we book the tickets and fly over to Greece under the vigilant eyes of their Gods and hope that Zeus doesn't send any thunderstorms our way during the flight.

After marveling at the beauty, we sail to Italy and move into the heart of Florence, where we acquaint ourselves with renaissance art and culture. Now, what do all these countries have in common?

They are all bordered by the Mediterranean Sea. That's how we got a geopolitical term that aims to encompass all our nourishment needs and set a quality standard for a healthy lifestyle.

To be precise, it is not just only one Mediterranean diet that is being eaten in all these countries. What is eaten varies greatly between countries in the Mediterranean.

There are also significant dietary variations within a region, such as in Italy. However, what is generally known as the Mediterranean-style diet has fruits, vegetables, breads and other cereals, breasts, nuts and seeds;

olive oil is a main source of fat; milk products; poultry and fish are consumed in small to moderate amounts; small red meat is consumed.

In search of the Mediterranean lifestyle

The Mediterranean diet is only one part of the Mediterranean lifestyle. Customs and traditions play a huge supporting role in a healthy lifestyle that is envied and adopted by people all over the world. So, what is it that people in the Mediterranean do differently than people elsewhere? It's simple. They're more connected to nature.

What do you picture when you think about the Mediterranean? Is it not the splendor that envelops the coast, auburn sundown with seagulls flying towards the horizon, and a soft breeze taking all your worries away? In general, the people in the Mediterranean lead a less stressful life because they realize the importance of slowing down to take a look around, in fear that they might miss it; miss life as it passes them by.

They dine outdoors because the weather permits them. They don't have to worry about cars pulling up in their driveways and exhausting fumes their way because the pollution is generally lesser in those areas. The people love to go for a stroll along the beaches, and this keeps them in shape even if they don't spend countless hours at the community gym. Their connectivity with nature goes far beyond their connectivity with electronic gadgets like mobile phones, computers, and television sets.

While people all over the world have grown addicted to the screens, it has resulted in a significant deterioration in their health and lifestyles. They have fallen sloth and are dragged into a state of monotony where ambitions no longer appeal to them. On the other hand, the Mediterranean people choose to give in to nature instead of routine.

We all remember the famous film quote from **The Godfather** *'In Sicily; women are more dangerous than shotguns.'* While that may be true for the 90s, the women and the men are definitely healthier in Sicily and other countries bordering the Mediterranean Sea.

Health benefits of the Mediterranean diet:

It's time we uncover what all the hype is about. The Mediterranean diet is largely famous for the massive health benefits that it entails. For starters, there's less risk of heart-related diseases, dementia, and depression. Think about it. Would you rather be sulking in your room all day eating ice-cream out of the carton or looking up recipes that actually banish the blues and lead to a healthier lifestyle enabling you to live your life to the fullest? I know for sure that I'd choose the latter.

The Mediterranean diet contains a significant spike in the intake of mono-saturated foods and omega 3s. There has been intensive research on the health benefits of omega 3s; healthy hair, baseline blood pressure, and an active lifestyle, and all you have to do is eat some salmon or any seafood or your choice because they are packed with the nutrient.

We also reduce the risk of cardiac and heart diseases by switching to this diet because we won't get the time or the munchies to consume processed foods at odd hours of the day. You won't just whip out a granola bar and start eating because the diet provides you with enough energy to get through the day. Using olive oil reduces the risk of high blood pressure and hypertension, so don't worry about the stress getting to you because all the natural palliatives in your diet are already working to keep it towards the back of your head.

Prevention is better than cure, right? You'd be surprised to know that the Mediterranean diet also reduces the risk of cancer because it includes a lot of plant-based foods that prevent the DNA from damage and stop cell mutation. They lower inflammation, so you needn't worry about apply any topical steroids to your scalp to combat dandruff because your diet will do that for you, targeting the root of the problem from the inside.

You won't ever have to worry about getting insulin injections on account of being diabetic or having to take PUGNAC, which is an insulin inhibitor. Your diet will automatically control the amount of insulin in your bloodstream and maintain healthy blood-glucose levels.

Numerous studies are linking certain mental illnesses to poor diets, and while this may come as a shock to you, it certainly doesn't affect you because the Mediterranean diet improves cognitive functions. The diet encourages nuts and yogurt, both of which preserve memory and improve your mood. So, if you've been getting the blues lately, then you should take a strong look at your dietary habits first.

Myths and facts about the Mediterranean diet

You know how we all love a good scandal and how pretentious some people are. 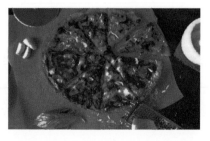 Put the two together, and we get a bunch of myths about almost everything there is. The

Mediterranean diet is no exception, so let's take a look at the absurd myths propagating around the diet that made its way overseas.

They say that **the Mediterranean diet does not work outside the Mediterranean**. While it is true that certain flavors are indeed exotic, it doesn't mean that they won't be available elsewhere. The modern world makes it a point to get products and people across state lines, so even if you don't find some of the products at your local grocery store, chances are you will find them at another. You might even come across someone who hails from the Mediterranean to bust the myths for you.

'The Mediterranean diet is all about pizza, pasta, and cheese.' This isn't that bad a myth considering Italy is one of the countries that border the Mediterranean Sea, and it's famous for some scrumptious pizza and pasta recipes, but a myth nonetheless.

As I stated before, a number of countries come under the

Mediterranean umbrella, and Italy is just one of them, so these delicacies are only there to complement the nuts and legumes, and also the vegetables and fruits.

'The Mediterranean diet is too high in fats.' I know we associate the word 'fats' with a potbelly, but the truth is that there are both healthy and unhealthy fats. The human body wouldn't be able to survive without fats because they are the energy reserves. The type of fats included in this diet is heart-healthy and does not cause weight gain, so there goes another myth. Busted!

'**You can't cook with extra virgin olive oil**.' This is actually my favorite myth because unhealthy and low-quality oils are used in many of the eastern countries like India, Pakistan, and Srilanka. It is rumored that virgin olive oil has a lower boiling point where it starts to break down, but that only happens with low-quality olive oil. Like everything else, olive-oil also comes in different qualities, and it takes a little trial and error before you come across the grocery aisle that contains high-quality olive oil.

'**The Mediterranean diet is hard to follow.**' This is the last of the urban myths on our list. Firstly, we need to understand that any diet is a little difficult to follow because changing your habits is an annoying process, and it's likely that you'll have to fight against some major cravings for unhealthy food.

The Mediterranean diet has a lot of variety, and these days, even seasonal foods are available all around the clock. The Mediterranean diet is focused on seasonal foods because the Mediterranean people have different eating habits. They eat very consciously so that they can actually taste and enjoy their food, whereas other people eat just for the sake of eating. All you have to do is pay a visit to your local farmer's market and pick out the ingredients.

Mediterranean Diet is helpful in losing weight

The versatile diet is not only recognized for being healthier, but it is also a well-documented fact that it promotes weight loss. This is due to the fact that the diet consists of water-rich foods, which refers to those items that fill up you very quickly when you've only taken a handful of bites. In recent times, obesity is on the rise, and every other commercial you see has a segment on some product that magically and drastically reduces weight.

These products are not only harmful to your health, but they are also very expensive, so even if they work, you have to ask yourself the cost at which you're losing weight. Industries have taken the opportunity to pursue the commodification of what the general public yearns for, and unfortunately, you have become just another in their grand scheme of things to earn money.

But all that ends today because we are going dive headfirst into how the Mediterranean diet is the best way to lose weight. The diet is so plentiful that you have a number of food choices to pick from in every department. You needn't force yourself to eat anything that you can't develop a taste for when there are so many alternatives available.

The key is to eat your food in small portions instead of taking three huge meals that fill you up to the brim. Imagine working long hours at the office, and your stomach starts growling way before the lunch break, so when you finally get off for the break, you eat more than necessary because you've been starving for a while. In this way, you consume more calories than required and end up contributing to that Christmas pot belly. To put the cherry on top, small meals keep you going throughout the day.

I emphasize that you have no obligation to try everything that is set on the dinner table. If you're having guests over and your wife has prepared a wide selection of delicacies, then try resisting the urge to put one of everything on your plate. Instead, eat two or three of the delectable items and leave more for the guests to savor. Also, don't forget to compliment your wife on preparing all that food! Trust me; it's not an easy task.

You've probably heard this one before, but it is essential that you drink more water. But why? How does water help in losing weight? Well, water carries out the toxins and fats stored in your body. Think of it like a stream that's constantly eroding a bluff, so each time a new wave comes, the bluff erodes further.

Now you drinking more water is like sending waves down your body that continue to erode the fat. Some people mistake drinking more for drinking more fluids, but if you start drinking more sodas or fizzy drinks, then you'll end up with a sore throat and a visit to the doctor. So always remember the complete phrase 'Drink more (water)'.

Never willfully deprive yourself of food so that you can starve to lose weight. It is not just unhealthy, but it also has other negative effects like reducing bone density, which means that you'll become more prone to injury, and it'll take longer to heal.

Going on the Mediterranean diet will speed your metabolism, which means that your body will burn calories faster. So, you will begin to lose weight naturally, which is a much better alternative to starving. It is documented that you can expect to lose two or more pounds weekly on the Mediterranean diet.

CHAPTER 2: HOW DOES MEDITERRANEAN DIET WORK?

The diet aims to change our eating habits. It focuses more on eating locally and seasonally so that your refrigerator is packed with the freshest of products. That said, you'll be making more trips to the local farmer's market than the local grocery store. To get a true sense of the diet, you have to savor the food.

Most people can't get through their meals without sitting in front of a television set, and more so, they rush to finish them. You have to take your time with the meal. Bite into it slowly and focus on the taste exploding inside your mouth. Let the smell of the food make you feel grateful to be alive. Eat with your friends and family instead of eating alone to share the joys of the Mediterranean lifestyle.

How to adopt a Mediterranean lifestyle?

The key to adopting the Mediterranean lifestyle is to familiarize yourself with the customs, traditions, and, most importantly, the eating habits of the Mediterranean people. This means that you have to acquaint yourself with the Mediterranean food pyramid.

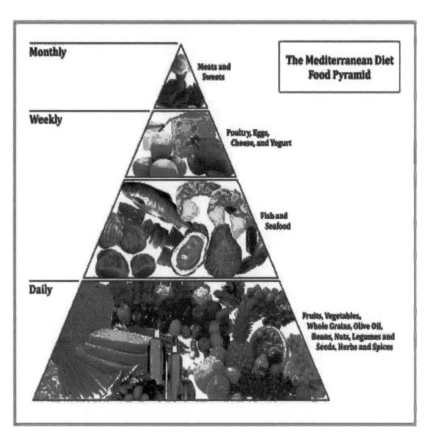

The bottom of the pyramid includes all sorts of whole-grain foods, fruits, vegetables and nuts and legumes that you can consume on a daily basis. Seafood and poultry can be consumed weekly, leaving meats and sweets for the last week of the month.

Adjusting to the lifestyle means cutting back on some unhealthy habits. Throw out all the stale food that is rotting inside the fridge and replace it with fresh products. Stop ordering takeout and lessen the visits to restaurants.

Most diners fry their products in unhealthy oils, and you can never gauge the freshness of the burgers when they're steaming hot. Wait for them to get cold, and only then are you able to be able to tell how fresh they really are.

The restaurant staff doesn't always focus all that much on hygiene, so who knows what kind of hands actually prepared your food and if they even wore gloves while preparing it? The Mediterranean diet prompts you to focus more on home-cooked meals that are clean and healthy.

You'll need to take another look at your cooking methods. Notice how you always eat deep-fried burgers when you go out? Sadly, that's no longer an option because deep-frying involves fats such as vegetables and peanut oils—no need to be alarmed though because there are plenty of other options available.

Roasting and steaming are the cooking methods that you should acquaint yourself with because they bring out all the flavor and none of the calories. Avoid boiling or simmering poultry and vegetables because these methods make the food lose most of their flavor and make the family think that you're following an impossible diet. Sautéing is great for foods that require minimal cooking time, such as mushrooms, leafy vegetables, and some shellfish. This method also uses minimal oil and evenly distributes the flavor. Sauté pans are used for this purpose.

Sticking to the diet

One of the major issues that most people face arrives when they get tired of sticking to a certain regime. So how does one will himself to stay committed? Before starting the diet, weigh the pros and cons for yourself. Do not go on a diet simply because a friend suggested or because you read the numerous benefits on the internet. It could already be that you have a healthy lifestyle, and a sudden change of habit might have a negative outcome on your health. A better option could be to familiarize yourself with the diet and integrate the beneficial aspects of your current lifestyle.

As Charles Bukowski once said, *'If you're going to try, go all the way. Otherwise, don't even start.'* Keep that in mind before starting, and if you feel like you're not too serious about the diet, then it might be better to start some other time. It's really no use if you drop the diet in between and relapse to your old eating habits. That could be even more harmful since your body was in the middle of adapting and might react unexpectedly if you abruptly change eating habits.

Find some support. If you're living with family, then tell them to motivate you when you're feeling down so that you don't end up going back on your diet. If you're living with a roommate, then convince him to start the diet with you so that both of you can keep prepping each other up along the way. If you're more of a loner like me, then you can hold yourself accountable for making any mistakes or erring on the course to a healthy lifestyle by reprimanding yourself.

No cheat meal days. Most people are under the impression that it's okay to have cheat meal days every once in a while, but what they don't realize is that the cheat days are minimal at first before they become a habit and lead the individual to ruin his entire diet plan.

Think of it like giving up smoking. If you kept going back for a cigarette once in a while, then you won't be able to quit now, would you?

Keep yourself busy. Find a hobby like gardening or writing a journal. Most people fall prey to temptation more easily when they have nothing to do and are more inclined in those moments to go back on their diet.

What food to eat?

As you've already studied the Mediterranean food pyramid, I'll summarize the guidelines to present a clearer image of what you can eat:

You can find a wide variety of fruits, vegetables, and whole grains

- Healthy fats, such as seeds, nuts, and olive oil
- Reasonable volumes of dairy and fish
- A very little amount of white meat and red meat
- Eggs
- Red wine not frequently

Let's dive further into the specifics.

- All sorts of vegetables are still on the table; Tomatoes, broccoli, kale, spinach, onions, cauliflower, carrots, Brussels sprouts, cucumbers, etc.
- Fruits are nature's gift to humanity, and you can reap all kinds; Apples, bananas, oranges, pears, strawberries, grapes, dates, figs, melons, peaches, etc.
- Don't be shy when it comes to nuts and seeds; Almonds, walnuts, macadamia nuts, hazelnuts, cashews, sunflower seeds, pumpkin seeds, etc.
- Legumes are your best friends now; Beans, peas, lentils, pulses, peanuts, chickpeas, etc.
- Tubers are vegetables that grow underground on the root of a plant, and they are especially high in fiber; Potatoes, sweet potatoes, turnips, yams, etc.
- Whole grains to meet your daily energy requirements; Whole oats, brown rice, rye, barley, corn, buckwheat, whole wheat, whole-grain bread, and pasta.
- Fish and seafood for a change; Salmon, sardines, trout, tuna, mackerel, shrimp, oysters, clams, crab, mussels, etc.
- Poultry for when the family comes over; Chicken, duck, turkey, etc.
- Eggs and egg-related dishes; Chicken, quail, and duck eggs.
- Dairy straight from the farm; Cheese, yogurt, Greek yogurt, etc.
- Herbs and spices add flavor to the food; Garlic, basil, mint, rosemary, sage, nutmeg, cinnamon, pepper, etc.
- Healthy fats to fill up on your energy reserves; Extra virgin olive oil, olives, avocados, and avocado oil.

All these foods have immense health benefits and will surely help you live a long and carefree life without any complications. You can also combine these ingredients to create mouth-watering recipes for breakfast, lunch, and dinner.

Getting used to different kinds of food

Are you a picky eater? Did you hate touching your veggies as a child? Yes. You thought that you'd never have to eat vegetables if you didn't want to, but now that you're older, you know that the key to a healthy life is a varied diet and it's that much difficult for you to get yourself to try new things because you still hate the leafy greens. It could be that you're not an avid foodie, so the question is, how do you successfully adopt a diet such as the Mediterranean diet when there are so many things in the food pyramid that you haven't tried?

The intuitive solution is to try something new at least once a week. There's a good chance you might hate it at first, but you have to develop a taste for new ingredients. It's a slow process, but over time, you'll get used to the variety of foods and start to enjoy eating them.

Start with foods placed at the bottom of the Mediterranean food pyramid and move towards the top. You'll find some food groups to satisfy you more than the others. This will help you compartmentalize them, and you'll also figure out your go-to choices in the pyramid.

What foods to avoid

There are certain restrictions when following any diet. You have to follow some rules, and I know they say 'rules are meant to be broken,' but you'll be better off if you don't break the rules of your diet by going anywhere near the off-limits food. So, let's have a quick look at the ingredients that are off-limits to you, effective immediately:

- Added sugar because you want your blood sugar levels to remain stable; Soda, candies, ice cream, table sugar, and many others.
- Refined grains because they contain empty calories; White bread, pasta made with refined wheat, etc.
- Trans fats because they increase the bad cholesterol in your system and lead to artery disease; Found in margarine and various processed foods.
- Refined oils because they have been refined by using chemicals that are harmful to us; Soybean oil, canola oil, cottonseed oil, and others.
- Processed meat because it puts you at a higher risk for heart disease; Processed sausages, hot dogs, etc.
- Highly processed foods that were made in factories; Anything labeled 'low-fat' or 'diet' or which looks like it was made in a factory.
- Butter because it contains saturated fats (almost 7 grams per tablespoon); Use olive oil instead, which is healthier and has less saturated fats (almost 2 grams per tablespoon).

It's common for us to overlook the ingredients plastered to the back of food labels, but you must carefully read food labels if you want to bypass these unhealthy ingredients.

What to drink

Water is at the top of the list, as you should aim to drink at least 64 ounces of water per day. If you get tired or feeling bore of drinking plain water, then try adding a squeeze of lemon juice, some slices of citrus fruits, or some berries to flavor the water and make it more refreshing and fuller of vitality.

The Mediterranean diet leaves room for a few casual drinks with food, and red wine is favored over the others. Other kinds of alcohol are still permitted so, but you can only consume 2 glasses per day if you want to remain guilt-free with respect to your diet. Don't worry about missing your daily morning boost and having dull mornings because **coffee** and **tea** are still acceptable. After all, isn't that what the tea leaves predicted?

You need to take a step back from artificial fruit juices because they are brimming with unreal sugar content. Carbonated drinks are also off-limits, and I doubt you'll feel the need for energy drinks unless you're addicted to one, in which case, you'll have to fight the urge.

Who says you can't enjoy a smoothie on a diet? The only difference will the preparation method and the addition of a few extra ingredients, for instance, a little Greek yogurt for protein and some nuts or avocados to increase the healthy fat content. Your smoothie will taste the same; only it'll fill you up and keep your blood sugar levels in check.

CHAPTER 3: BREAKFAST MEDITERRANEAN DIET RECIPE

It seems a little dry, doesn't it? But that's only the illusion and it's going to shatter this very second because I'm going to give you a number of mouth-watering recipes for your breakfast, lunch, and dinner based on this diet.

The Mediterranean diet has numerous health benefits, in particular in reducing the chances of heart attacks and strokes. But even if you are not worried about your heart health and just want to eat better, follow the Mediterranean diet may be worth considering.

According to the research, the Mediterranean diet is mostly plant-based diet. Fruit, vegetables, pulses, and whole grains, and substitutes butter with 'good fats including olive oil and canola oil,' walnuts, figs, and tomatoes you like, with even a little feta cheese or Greek yogurt. So, if you are looking for some breakfast recipe, here are some for your help!

1. Shakshuka

Shakshuka is a Traditional Mediterranean Breakfast recipe in tomato pepper sauce with poached eggs. There are several definitions of Shakshuka recipe, but it's literally a bell pepper with tomato sauce with poached eggs. It's a very easy and quick recipe. Let's see how we will make it!

Cooking time: 20 minutes

Ingredients

- 2 small size Onion
- 2 cloves of Garlic
- Half piece of Ginger
- 2 small size Tomatoes
- 1 bell pepper
- 3 eggs
- Salt to taste

- Black pepper to taste
- Sugar to taste
- Olive oil

Instruction

- Place a medium-size fry pan on the stove and heat it over slow to medium heat.
- Add oil and sautés onions with peppers.
- Add crushed Garlic, tomatoes, and sugar.
- Cook the onion and tomatoes for 5 minutes and then add salt and pepper.
- Now make 4 little indentations and crack the eggs in the pan.
- Cover and cook until the eggs have only been set.

This part is important because egg should not be overcooked. Keep the flame low and cover it. In minutes, it is difficult to determine as it depends on the size of the eggs and how the egg spreads. Check every 2 minutes and take the cover off and remove from the heat if you see that egg whites are set up.

Serve it with bread.

2. Healthy Quick Breakfast Sandwich

A very easy and quick breakfast recipe is here. Let's find out how we will make it!

Cooking time: 20 minutes

Ingredients

- 2 slice of sandwich bread
- 2 Egg
- 1 teaspoon olive oil
- Salt to taste
- Black pepper to taste
- Half cup Spanish leaves
- 1 small size Tomatoes (cut in a slice)
- One slice Feta Cheese

Instruction

- Place a medium-size pan over the stove and heat it for 5 minutes
- Place sandwich bread and add half teaspoon of olive oil.
- Toast them for 5 minutes from both sides.
- Now take a small bowl and add eggs and salt and pepper and mix them.
- Now take another pan and heat it over small heat. Now add the egg mixture in it and cook it for about 5 minutes from both sides.

- Now place sandwich bread on a plate and place Spanish leaves.
- Place tomatoes slice and then omelet.
- Place cheese.
- Top it with another slice.

A sandwich is ready to serve.

3. Baked Egg with Avocado

This Baked Eggs with Avocado and Feta is an outstanding and easy breakfast recipe for people, who are avocado lovers, which you know is also low in carbs. So, let's find out more about it.

Cooking time: 25 minutes

Ingredients

- 2 Eggs
- 1 avocado (cut in thin slice)
- Salt to taste
- Black pepper to taste
- Feta cheese

Instructions

- Take two bowls and spray them with olive oil.

- Now peel the avocado and cut it into thin slice.
- Place avocado in each bowl.
- Now break both eggs and put them over avocado carefully.
- Sprinkle salt and pepper over them.
- Now place some feta cheese over them.
- Bake them for 15 minutes in a preheated oven.

Serve them with bread.

4. Egg with Olive and Tomatoes

If you are looking for a fast, protein-packed Mediterranean Diet breakfast recipe, then this recipe is for you. Start your morning with delicious Eggs and Tomatoes. This delicious breakfast has some of the most nutritious ingredients in the Mediterranean. Let's find out about its ingredients and instructions.

Cooking Time: 15 minutes

Ingredients

- 5 Greek olives
- 2 Eggs
- 2 Tomatoes
- Half cup Feta Cheese
- Salt to taste

- Black pepper to taste

Instructions

- Place a large frying pan on a stove for 5 minutes over small heat.
- Add the tomatoes in olive oil for 10 minutes and sauté them.
- Add the olives and cook for about 5 minutes.
- Whisk the eggs in a small bowl with salt and pepper and add egg mixture to the frying pan.
- Cook eggs over medium heat until they start to set.
- Add feta cheese.
- Cook them as you like.

Serve them hot

5. Creamy oatmeal bowls with raspberry seeds and honey

Let's start with the **ingredients:**

- You're going to need 1 cup of rolled oats,
- ½ teaspoon of ground cinnamon,
- 2 cups of boiling water,
- two teaspoons butter, and
- A pinch of salt.

- You can have toppings of your choice, but I recommend fresh berries, seeds, and nuts of your choice and honey to taste.

Directions:

Take some oats in the saucepan as you turn the heat to moderate temperature and then add water and sauce to bring to a boil. Add the oats and then cook for about 5 minutes. Lower the heat and allow the mixture to simmer for 10 minutes as you stir steadily until the oats get creamy and the water well absorbed. Take the saucepan off from the burner and place the oats in a pot. Add cinnamon and butter, and cover with a lid as you allow to cook for 5 minutes. Stir the oats again once the time has elapsed and then serve with your favorite toppings.

6. Spanish Mediterranean Omelet

This is the best and delicious omelet recipe! Enjoy it in your breakfast, and start your day with the right energy dishes. While I typically avoid potatoes because of their high (sugar) load; however, they give a good source of fiber and nutrients in this dish. Let's find out more about this dish.

Cooking time: 30 minutes

Ingredients

- 2 eggs
- 2 small size Potatoes
- 1 small onion
- 1 small Tomato
- 4 tablespoon Olive oil
- Salt to taste
- Black pepper to taste
- Half cup of Spanish

Instructions

- Heat a medium-size frypan over medium heat for 5 minutes.
- Add 2 tablespoons of olive oil; add the potatoes, onion, and tomato, then cook for about 15 minutes until the mixture is cook.
- Meantime, you can whisk the eggs in a large bowl with the salt, pepper.
- Spoon the potato blend with the eggs in the bowl and combine well.

- Take the same pan and heat it over medium heat and add the other 2 tablespoons of olive oil. Put the mixture of egg and potato in the pan, cover, over medium heat, and cook for about 5 minutes.
- Check after 5 minutes if the eggs are done, and the bottom is golden, turn the omelet over a plate, move it back into the pan and cook again for a few minutes.
- Serve them hot with your favorite bread.

CHAPTER 4: MEDITERRANEAN DIET LUNCH RECIPES

In the morning, making your own lunch saves money, and can be much safer. You will not miss these special lunch recipes when consuming Mediterranean food (including all tomatoes, lemons, feta, and olives you can put on a plate for lunch. Instead of watching people trying, you should try out the Mediterranean diet is a century lifestyle for long-term health and wellbeing rather than an easy weight loss trend that never seems to last.

The Mediterranean diet includes olive oils as well as vegetables, beans, legumes, nuts, and seeds. There is also a fish on the menu, with sprinkles of cheese. Research shows that the Mediterranean diet can minimize the risk of cardiovascular disease, increase fat loss, and safeguard against type 2 diabetes. Here are some lunch recipes for your kitchen.

1. Best Lentil Soup

Lentil is usually low in calories, nutritious, and budget-friendly, and its recipe is very easy and quick. And here's our favorite new way of eating them. This vegan lentil soup is full of great flavor, with just herb and less spice.

Cooking Time: 60 minutes

Ingredients

- 2 small size onions
- 1 medium-size Carrot
- 2 cloves of Garlic
- Half piece gingers
- 1 cup Green lentil
- Salt to taste
- Black pepper to taste
- ¼ cup olive oil
- 3 small size tomato
- 1 cup of water
- 2 cup Spanish
- 1 teaspoon oregano

Instructions

- Peel the carrots and cut them into slice.
- Crush the Ginger and Garlic and stir as soon as the soup is prepared.

- Sock them into the water for about half-hour
- Take a medium size pressure cooker and heat the olive oil over medium heat.
- Add onion and sauté until they become brown for 6 to 7 minutes.
- Add carrots, lentils, tomatoes, water, salt, peppers, and oregano.
- Cook it for about 40 minutes.

Serve hot!

2. Mediterranean Baked Chicken with Salad

These delicious baked chicken breasts in the oven, mixing Mediterranean salads with vegetables, and simple homemade Greek dressing for a weekend in less than an hour will be the best choice for lunch. Let's find out what is its recipe.

Cooking Time: 45 minutes

Ingredients

- 3 boneless chicken Breast pieces
- 2 tablespoon olive oil
- ½ teaspoon lemon zest
- Salt to taste
- Black pepper to taste
- ½ cup Spanish
- 1 small size cucumber (chopped)

- 1 small size Carrot (chopped)
- I small size onion (chopped)
- I small size Tomato (chopped)
- ¼ cup feta cheese

Instructions

- Preheat oven to 375 degrees.
- Take a plate and add chicken breast over it.
- Brush with one tablespoon oil and sprinkle the salt and pepper with lemon and 1/4 teaspoon.
- Place in a baking dish.
- Bake for about 30 minutes until it cooks well from both sides.
- Meanwhile, add water in a saucepan to a boil over high heat.
- Add spinach and cook for 5 minutes.
- Coldwater drain and rinse.
- Drain well and transfer into a dish. Stir in cucumber, onions, tomato, feta, and olives.
- In a small bowl, beat two tablespoons of oil, lemon juice, garlic, oregano.
- Add this dressing in salad and mix it.

Rub the remaining dressing over the chicken and serve with the salad.

3. Spanish Soup with Chicken and Beans

This aromatic Mediterranean soup recipe with few ingredients such as a boneless, skinless chicken breast, spinach, and canned beans will be a good addition in your Mediterranean diet cookbook. It is a very easy and quick recipe. Let's find out about its ingredients and instructions.

Cooking time: 30 minutes

Ingredients

- 1 tablespoon olive oil
- ¼ cup carrot
- 1 clove of Garlic
- 1 small size boneless chicken breast
- 3 cups chicken broth
- ½ cup Spanish
- Salt to taste
- Black pepper to taste
- 1 can of beans
- ¼ cup cheese

Instructions

- Take a large pot, and add 1 teaspoon of oil over medium-high.

- Add the carrot and chicken turn the chicken and frequently stir until it became brown for about 5 minutes.
- Add Garlic, stirring, and cook for 2 minutes.
- Add chicken broth and boil it.
- Reduce heat and stir until the chicken is cooked for about five minutes.
- Take out chicken pieces with a spoon to a clean cutting board to cool.
- Add spinach, beans, and boil to the pot.
- Cook for 5 minutes.
- Break the chicken into a small size. In the bowl, add the chicken. Sprinkle salt and pepper.

Add cheese and serve hot.

4. Lemon Chicken Skewers with Special Yogurt Sauce

A very interesting and delicious recipe for your menu is here. This quick and healthy Mediterranean tastes blended well with a salad and serves it with white pita bread. Best of all, it will take only 50 minutes to cook.

Cooking Time: 50 minutes

Ingredients

- 4 Skewers
- 1 lemon juice

- ½ teaspoon oregano
- 2 medium-size chicken breasts (cut into small pieces)
- Salt to taste
- Black pepper to taste
- 1 teaspoon garlic powder
- 1 teaspoon ginger powder
- 1 tablespoon olive oil
- ¼ cup curd

For sauce

- ½ cup curd
- 1 teaspoon lemon juice
- ½ cucumber (cut in small size)
- 1 teaspoon garlic powder
- 1 teaspoon ginger powder
- Salt to taste
- Black pepper to taste

Instructions

- Take a small bowl and add yogurt, cucumber, salt, black pepper, 1 teaspoon of lemon juice, I teaspoon of ginger and garlic powder, and mix them for 5 minutes. Sauce is ready!

- Now take another bowl and add yogurt, salt, black pepper powder, lemon juice, and oregano. Now mix them and set aside.
- Take another plate and add chicken and rub it with yogurt sauce you just made.
- Place two-piece on each skewer and brush them with olive oil. Cook them on the hot grill pan for about 5 minutes from both sides or until they change their color.

Serve with Tzatziki sauce.

5. Mediterranean Chickpea and Chicken Soup

This is a very interesting and easy recipe for your Mediterranean lunch menu. This soup is cook in a slow cooker for about 4 hours. Let's find out more about it.

Cooking time: 4 hours

Ingredients

- ½ cup chickpea (soaked overnight)
- 4 pieces of chicken leg
- 1 medium-size onion
- 5 cups of water
- Salt to taste
- Black pepper to taste

- 1 tablespoon tomato paste
- 1 medium-size tomato (cut in slices)
- 3 cloves of Garlic (chopped)
- 1 teaspoon cumin seeds
- ¼ cup of olive

Instructions

- Soak chickpeas overnight in water
- Take a small size slow cooker and add soaked chickpeas, salt, tomato, water, onion, cumin seed, black pepper, and chicken.
- Stir them for 2 minutes.
- Cover and cook the soup for about 4 hours over a high flame.
- After four hours, remove the cooker from heat and transfer the chicken on a plate.
- Shred the chicken
- Now add olives and shredded chicken.

Serve hot

6. Lemon Chicken with Noodles

This Lemon Parmesan Chicken and Zucchini Noodles is a great meal, which is quick and spiced! It is a great pasta chicken, very light, low carb, and so easy to cook. Let's find out more about it.

Cooking Time: 20 minutes

Ingredients

- 1 packet frozen green vegetable
- 1 breast of chicken (cut into thin slice)
- Salt to taste
- Black pepper to taste
- 2 teaspoon olive oil
- 3 cloves of Garlic (chopped)
- 1 teaspoon oregano

- 1 tablespoon lemon juice
- 2 cups of chicken broth
- ½ cup parmesan cheese
- 1 pack of noodles
- 1 tablespoon of butter

Instructions

- Cook noodles as per box instructions. Drain well.
- Oil must be heated on medium heat in a large cooking pot.
- Season chicken with salt and green veggies and cook them over medium heat until they become brown, depending on the thickness approximately 4 minutes per side.

- Add Garlic to the pot and cook for about 30 seconds until it changes color.
- Add butter and lemon juice, oregano, salt, and pepper and cook it.
- Add chicken broth and mix it carefully until all mix well.
- Change heat into the medium from high to boil chicken and sauce.
- Remove the pan after 20 mins, from the heat immediately and pour in the parmesan cheese.
- Put the chicken back in a pot and cook for 5 minutes, or until the sauce is slightly thickened.

Serve it hot over noodles.

7. Grilled Chicken with Cauliflower Rice

This is a very healthy and balanced Mediterranean recipe included bowls of rice, topped with feta cheese, olives, vegetables, and grilled chicken is impressive. It will take only 30 minutes to cook. Let's find out more about this easy recipe.

Cooking time: 30 minutes

Ingredients

- 1 tablespoon olive oil
- 2 cups cauliflower rice

- 1 small size onion
- 2 boneless chicken breasts
- Salt to taste
- Black pepper to taste
- 1 tablespoon of lemon juice
- 1 teaspoon butter
- ½ teaspoon of oregano
- 1 small size tomato
- 1 small size cucumber
- ½ cup of olive
- ½ cup of Feta cheese

Instructions

- Preheat a medium-size grill.
- Heat the 1/2 tablespoon of olive oil on medium heat in a large pot. Add cauliflower rice, onion, salt, and black pepper powder.
- Cook, about 5 minutes until cauliflower rice softens.
- Take ½ tablespoon of olive oil and rub it over the chicken.
- Mix 1/2 teaspoon of salt and 1/2 teaspoon of pepper.
- Grill about 15 minutes in all, Whisk the rest of the 1 tablespoons butter, lemon juice, oregano in a small bowl with salt and pepper.

- Divide the rice into 4 cups: spread chicken, onions, cucumber, feta, and olives.
- Add the dressing.

Serve them hot.

CHAPTER 5: MEDITERRANEAN DIET DINNER RECIPES

Dinner is a perfect time to branch out and try a new recipe while adopting the Mediterranean diet lifestyle. A key part of the Mediterranean diet plan is eating fish once or twice a week.

This Mediterranean diet is also one of the healthiest diets that you can try, whether to lose weight or control blood sugar levels better. If you want to combine the concepts with quick recipes, such as low-carb recipes, you can also try the following recipes to avoid the same recipes for dinner.

1. Stuffed Chicken Breasts

This easy recipe of stuffed chicken breast with Spanish and feta cheese is very healthy. It is also a quick recipe made in 1 hour. You will bake it for 30 minutes in the oven. Let's find out more about it!

Cooking time: 1 hour

Ingredients

- 1 tablespoon olive oil
- ¼ cup feta cheese
- ¼ cup Spanish
- ¼ cup red bell pepper
- ¼ cup olives
- Salt to taste
- Black pepper to taste
- 2 cloves of Garlic
- 2 small size chicken breasts (cut into thin slice)

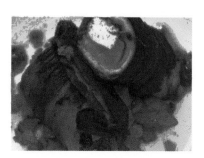

Instructions

- Preheat oven at 275 degree
- Take a small bowl and add bell pepper, olives, Spanish, salt, Garlic, and black pepper.
- Take a knife and cut a chicken from the middle to make a small pocket.
- Stuff chicken with the mixture.
- Sprinkle salt and black pepper over it.
- Take a small fry pan and place it over medium heat and heat 1 teaspoon olive oil.
- Place chicken breast pocket over it and cook them until they become brown from both sides.

- Remove the pan and place it inside the preheated oven.
- Bake it for about half an hour.

Serve it hot.

2. Time to share the best way of

Ingredients

- Trim or peel the veggies as needed
- Line a baking sheet or dish with foil and add a quarter-sized portion of olive oil.

- Dump in the veggies and mix them with your clean hands until they are well coated.
- Rub the oil into the backs of your hands before rinsing and then add salt, pepper, and any other seasonings.

Instructions

Roast the required time (usually 10-30 minutes depending on the vegetable and the size of the pieces), place into a serving dish or your plate, and then throw away the foil.'

And what do you know; you have now cooked your veggies the Mediterranean way.

3. Salmon fish with Spanish leaves

A very easy and interesting recipe for your dinner menu is here. Easy to make with a few ingredients. Very quick to make in less than 20 minutes.

Cooking time: 15 minutes

Ingredients

- 2 Salmon fish fillets
- Salt to taste
- Black pepper to taste
- 2 tablespoon of olive oil
- ½ cup Spanish leaves
- 2 cloves of Garlic (crushed)

Instructions

- Preheat grill.
- Mix a pinch of salt and black pepper in olive oil. Rub this olive oil over fish fillets. Place them on a griller.
- Cook it for about 5 minutes from both sides until it cooks well.
- Meanwhile, heat remaining oil in a large cooking pan over medium heat. Add Garlic, or cook until fragrant for 15 seconds.

- Now add chopped Spanish leave in it and cook it for about 3 minutes.
- Take out this mixture from pan and place it on the plate.

Serve fish fillet over it.

4. Mediterranean chicken Stuffed Pepper

These Mediterranean Stuffed peppers are such a great recipe and filled with fatty foods. But with all the flavors of the ingredients, this version of the recipe is light and new. We will add Sweet lemon, peppery oregano, spicy tomatoes as filling.

Cooking time: 30 minutes

Ingredients

- 1 piece of chicken breast (cut into thin slices)
- 1 small size onion
- 4 medium-size tomatoes
- 3 small size olives
- 1 teaspoon oregano
- 3 bell pepper
- Salt to taste
- Black pepper to taste

- Feta cheese

Instructions

- Preheat the oven at 350
- Take a pan and place it on the oven and heat it over medium heat.
- Now add chicken slices and fry it in 1 tablespoon of olive oil. Cook it until it changes its color to brown.
- Cut the peppers in two halves and remove the seeds.
- Spray the olive oil and salt and pepper in the peppers. Place in the oven for 5 minutes on a baking tray to soften.
- Chop the onion, tomatoes, olives, and herbs. Stir the lemon and add cooked chicken chunks and stuff mixture in the peppers and bake them about 15 minutes in the oven.
- After 15 minutes, add cheese slices and keep those in the oven until it melts.

Serve pepper hot.

5. Quinoa and Vegetable Soup

With a large number of vegetables, this delicious quinoa vegetable soup offers a wide variety of nutrients and is a very healthy recipe. In this aromatic soup, you will taste little sweet potatoes, sprouts in Brussels, celery root, and more veggies with quinoa. Let's find out more about it.

Cooking time: 60 minutes

Ingredients

- ½ cup quinoa
- 4 teaspoon olive oil
- 1 small size onion (chopped)
- 1 small size carrot (chopped)
- 1 small size green bell pepper (chopped)
- 2 cloves of Garlic (chopped)
- 1 teaspoon cumin seeds
- 1 teaspoon rosemary
- Salt to taste
- Black pepper to taste
- 3 cups of chicken stock

- 2 small size potato (chopped)
- 2 small size sweet potato (chopped)

Instruction

- Preheat the oven to 275 degrees.
- Take one pack of and Spread it on a baking sheet in a thin layer; bake it at 275 degrees for about 30 minutes until browned.
- Heat a big medium cooking pot over medium heat.

- Add all the vegetables and chicken stock. Cover the cooking pot tightly and cook for 10 minutes, or until vegetables are tender, stirring occasionally.
- Add salt and pepper and then whisk in rosemary and cumin.
- Add toasted quinoa and Increase heat to high and boil the soup.
- After 5 minutes, cover and change the heat to medium and cook for 12 minutes.

Soup is ready.

Serve it hot

6. Mediterranean Chicken

You can't have lunch without chicken, can you? The ingredients are relatively fewer for this one as the only things you'll need.

Ingredients:

- 4 boneless chicken breast halves
- ¼ teaspoon pepper and salt
- 3 tablespoons of olive oil
- 1 pint of grape tomatoes
- 16 ripe olives
- 3 tablespoons of drained capers

Directions:

- Sprinkle salt and pepper on the chicken.
- Place a skillet over medium heat and cook the chicken for 3 minutes on each side or until golden brown.
- Add some olives, tomatoes, and capers.
- Set the oven to 475 F and let it sit for 15 minutes.
- Remove from the oven once ready, and the fragrance will indicate that your chicken is completely cooked and ready to serve.

7. Slow cooker pasta with Chicken and Beans

Try this new slow-cooked classic recipe on a family weekend dinner with this Pasta, chicken, and beans. We will also add tomatoes, feta cheese, herbs, pasta, and beans all simmered together in a pot to make a good, moist soup cup. Serve with a slice of bread and cheese. Let's find out more about it.

Cooking Time: 60 minutes

Ingredients

- One packet of pasta
- One boneless chicken breast piece (cut into small chunks)
- One can of beans
- Salt to taste
- Black pepper to taste

- 2 small size tomato (chopped)
- 2 small size onion (chopped)
- 1 clove of Garlic (chopped)
- 2 small piece of feta cheese
- One teaspoon oregano
- One teaspoon cumin seed
- Crushed red pepper
- 3 tablespoon olive oil
- 5 cups of water

Instructions

- Take a slow cooker and place it on the stove and heat it.
- Add olive oil and chicken piece chunks and fry them until they become brown.
- Now add all the ingredients like tomato, garlic, onion, salt, and pepper and fry them with chicken for about 5 minutes.
- Now add 5 cups of water and mix them—Cook this soup for about 50 minutes.
- After 50 minutes, open the cooker cover and add cumin seed, feta cheese, and oregano.
- Now take another cooking pot and boil the pasta according to packet instructions.

- Add the boil pasta and bean into chicken soup. Sprinkle the crushed red chili.

Serve soup hot.

8. Baked Salmon with white rice

Baked salmon fish is one of the best recipes for your dinner menu. It is light and easy to cook. Great for your weekend or all year round! Baked Herbed Salmon! A Simple salmon covered with some herbs and baked to make dinner healthy. Let's find out more about it!

Cooking time: 25 minutes

Ingredients

- 2 cups of rice
- 3 salmon fish fillets
- Salt to taste
- Black pepper to taste
- 1 tablespoon of olive oil
- 1 teaspoon of rose marry
- 1 teaspoon oregano
- 1 lemon

Instructions

- Preheat oven at 275 degree
- Spread a foil pepper on a baking tray.

- Take a bowl and mix lemon juice, salt, black pepper, oregano, and rosemary with 1 tablespoon of olive oil.
- Now rub this dressing over fish evenly and keep it in the fridge for about 1 hour.
- After 1 hour, bake it for about 15 minutes.
- Boil the rice and serve the fish with rice.

9. Mediterranean Buttermilk Chicken with rice

Buttermilk Mediterranean Chicken is a very easy and quick recipe. This is a very simple recipe with a few ingredients such as Garlic, salt, black pepper, buttermilk, etc. You will be able to cook it in less than one hour.

Cooking time: 1 hour

Ingredients

- 2 small boneless chicken breast pieces
- 3 cloves of Garlic
- Salt to taste
- Black pepper to taste
- ½ cup of buttermilk
- 1 teaspoon cumin seeds
- 1 teaspoon oregano
- 2 tablespoon olive oil

Instructions

- Take a bowl and add buttermilk with salt, black pepper, garlic, cumin, and oregano.
- Mix it for about two minutes and add chicken breast in this mixture.
- Keep aside the chicken for 30 minutes in the room fridge.
- Now take a grill pan and place it over a stove and heat it at medium flame.
- Add olive oil and add chicken breast and cook them from both sides for about 10 minutes.
- Remove the pan from heat when chicken becomes brown from both sides and cook well.

Serve the chicken breast hot.

10. Chicken Burger with tahini sauce

Red meat is not part of the Mediterranean diet exactly, but fish and chicken are! Next time you have a craving for having a burger, you can try to lay this light chicken burger. With tomatoes, feta, and red onions, it is much more flavorful than even ordinary hamburgers, and a delighted part of the recipe is adding of ketchup and mayo is the creamy tahini sauce.

Cooking time: 1 hour

Ingredients

- 2 boneless chicken breasts

- 1 packet of burger
- 1 tablespoon olive oil
- Salt to taste
- Black pepper to taste
- 1 small size tomato (cut into slice)
- 1 small size onion (cut into slice)

Sauce

- ½ cup curd
- 1 teaspoon lemon juice
- ½ cucumber (cut in small size)
- 1 teaspoon garlic powder
- 1 teaspoon ginger powder
- Salt to taste
- Black pepper to taste
- 1 tablespoon of ketchup
- 1 tablespoon mayonnaise

Instructions

- Pan must be heated over medium heat for about 5 minutes.
- Add olive oil and heat it.
- Place chicken fillet and fry it from both sides. Sprinkle salt and pepper over it.

63

- Cook it until it becomes brown or cook well.
- Take a pan and heat it over slow heat and place burger and toast them from both sides.
- Take a bowl and add yogurt with salt, black pepper, garlic and ginger powder, and lemon juice. Add one tablespoon of ketchup and mayonnaise in this sauce.
- Now place chicken fillet over a burger.
- Place slice of tomato and onion over it.
- Spread one tablespoon of sauce over the burger.
- Cover it with another part of a burger bun.

Serve burger hot with sauce.

11. Feta Shrimp Skillet

As we notice more sunshine getting in through the windows, let's talk about lunch. I present you with a feta shrimp skillet to satiate all your mid-day cravings.

Ingredients:

You're going to need

- 1 tablespoon of olive oil
- 1 finely chopped medium onion
- 3 minced garlic cloves
- ½ teaspoon of pepper

- 2 cans of diced tomatoes
- 1 pound of uncooked shrimp peeled and deveined
- 2 tablespoons of minced fresh parsley
- ¾ cup of crumbled feta cheese
- 1 teaspoon of dried oregano and pepper and some salt to taste

Directions:

- Place a large non-stick skillet over moderate heat and then add oil.
- Add finely chopped onion.
- Cook for about 4 minutes as you occasionally stir.
- Add seasonings and garlic, and then cook for one more minute.
- Stir in tomatoes as you wish. After this, bring to a boil.
- Decrease heat and then allow to cook for 7 minutes without the lid or until the sauce is thickened.
- Add shrimp and parsley and cook for 6 minutes or until shrimp turns pink as you occasionally stir.

- Remove from heat once cooked and then sprinkle with cheese and let it remain covered for some time until the cheese softens.

Say grace and serve.

CHAPTER 6: SIX DELICIOUS SALAD RECIPES

Would you like to eat the Mediterranean way? Mediterranean diet is very useful for weight loss. It has gained fame as one of the world's healthiest diets. And it is not typical dietary food, people: Mediterranean diet recipes are real, fresh, and really delicious. Why we love it even more? It's not just food: it's an approach to lifestyle. Here I gathered a collection of some of our favorite healthy salad recipes.

1. Mediterranean Tuna salad

If you are fed up from having the same mayo-heavy tuna salads, then try this safe and radiant tuna salad!

You can prepare with crunchy vegetables, like celery, cucumbers, new herbs and onions, and Dijon dressing.

Cooking time: 15 minutes

Ingredients

- Dijon dressing
- 1 tablespoon mustard paste
- 1 tablespoon lime juice
- 1 tablespoon olive oil
- Salt to taste
- Black pepper to taste
- Tuna
- 1 can tuna
- 1 small size cucumber
- 2 celery stalks
- 3 small size radishes
- 2 small size onion
- ½ cup olives
- 10 mint leaves
- 1 bunch of parsley
- 2 small size tomato

Instructions

- Take a bowl and add mustard paste, lime juice, olive oil, salt, and black pepper. Mix this mixture carefully.
- Cut and chopped all vegetables.

- Take a plate and add tuna and all vegetables.
- Pour the dressing over salad and mix it.

Serve it with dinner.

2. Mediterranean Green Salad

This green Mediterranean Salad makes a perfect recipe for a light meal or an enjoyable side dish. Get this simple, stylish Mediterranean salad recipe and make your dinner or lunch memorable.

Preparation time: 10 minutes

Ingredients

3 cups of green salad

Salt to taste

Black pepper to taste

- 1 small size tomato (chopped)
- 1 small size onion (chopped)
- 1 small size green onion (chopped)
- 1 small size radish (chopped)
- 1 small size cucumber (chopped)
- ½ cup feta cheese

Instructions

- Take a large size plate and add all the chopped vegetables with green salad and salt and pepper.
- Mix the salad well
- Add feta cheese on top and serve as a side dish with lunch or dinner.

3. Hard-Boiled Egg and tuna salad

This salad is very healthy and quick to make also. It's a real treat, a healthy Mediterranean diet that you're going to eat for days. This salad has ingredients such as boiled eggs, green bean, olives, tomatoes, and potato salads that are filled with crunchy lettuce. It is enough to be the main dish. Let's find out more about it.

Preparation time: 10 minutes

Ingredients

- 1 ounce of lettuce
- 2 eggs (boil)
- 1 can of Tuna
- Salt to taste
- Black pepper to taste
- 1 small size potato (boil)
- 1 small size tomato (chopped)
- 1 small size red onion (chopped)
- ½ cup of olives (chopped)

Instructions

- Boil the egg and potato.
- Take a large size plate and add tuna and all veggies with egg and salt and pepper.
- Mix the salad well and serve it in serving dish with lunch or dinner.

4. Mediterranean Bean Salad

If you want to lose weight? You can serve this salad as the main meal with grilled salmon, lamb or chicken, and with a small piece of bread. This is a simple and speedy recipe.

Cooking time: 10 minutes

Ingredients

- 1 medium-size onion (chopped)
- 1 medium-size carrot (chopped)
- 1 medium-size radish (chopped)

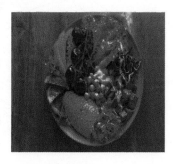

- 1 medium-size cucumber (chopped)
- 3 medium-size tomato (chopped)
- ½ cup olive (chopped)
- 1 can of bean (rinsed and boil)

71

- 1 small size capsicum (chopped)
- 1 tablespoon olive oil
- 1 tablespoon lemon juice
- Salt to taste
- Black pepper to taste
- Mint leaves
- ½ cup Feta cheese

Instructions

- Add the ingredients in a bowl and mix them with a fork.
- Now take a small bowl and add olive oil, lemon juice, salt, and pepper and mix this sauce.
- Add the dressing into a salad bowl and mix it.
- Serve the salad with lunch and dinner.

5. Chickpea Salad with Oregano Dressing

This salad has a perfect balance: protein-packed chickpeas add amazing taste; however, all crunchy veggies give it a texture and keep it sweet. And it is easy to eat by cutting it in small bits and ensuring that you get a little of it all with every bite.

Cooking time: 20 minutes

Ingredients

Dressing

- 2 cloves of Garlic (chopped)

- 1 tablespoon of mustard paste
- 1 tablespoon of olive oil
- 1 tablespoon vinegar
- Salt to taste
- Black pepper to taste
- 1 teaspoon oregano

Salad

- 1 cup Chickpea (boil)
- I small size onion (chopped)
- 1 small size cucumber (chopped)
- 1 small bell pepper (chopped)
- 1 small radish (chopped)

- Salt to taste
- Black pepper to taste
- ½ cup feta cheese
- 10 mint leaves
- 1 iceberg lettuce

Instructions

- Add mustard paste, olive oil, vinegar, oregano, salt, and pepper and mix this dressing in a bowl.

- Keep this sauce in the fridge for a half-hour.
- Now take another bowl and add all the chopped ingredients with chickpeas.
- Mix all the ingredients for 1 minute.
- Add the sauce into salad before serving and mix it carefully.
- Now take ice burg lettuce and chop it and mix it into salad.

Serve the salad with lunch or dinner as you like.

6. Cauliflower Salad

This salad recipe is unique and interesting. It is loaded with fresh summer veggies and is vegan, gluten-free, and perfect for a diet. The Mediterranean diet has nothing against carbohydrates, but you can choose this salad as long as you want to avoid taking carbohydrates. Cauliflower was microwaved until tender, then mix with a heap of other vegetables and dressing. You're going to feel like you are eating rice, but it's really a vegetable.

Cooking time: 20 minutes

Ingredients

- 1 small size cauliflower
- I small size onion (chopped)

- 1 small size cucumber (chopped)
- 1 small bell pepper (chopped)
- 1 small radish (chopped)
- Salt to taste
- Black pepper to taste
- 1 tablespoon olive oil
- 1 tablespoon lemon juice
- ½ cup feta cheese
- 10 mint leaves

Instructions

- Take a cutting board and chop the cauliflower with a knife.
- Now preheat the oven and take a baking tray and add this cauliflower and bake it for 2 minutes.
- Take a separate bowl and add all the chopped vegetables and mix them.
  - Add olive oil, lemon juice, salt, and pepper in this salad and mix it.
- Add crunch cauliflower in the salad and mix it.

It is ready to serve.

CONCLUSION

The Mediterranean diet is one of the best out there because it offers a versatile food pyramid, and with minimal restrictions, you won't feel overwhelmed while adjusting to it. The notion of the Mediterranean people is to turn mealtime into quality time with friends and family; to consciously enjoy and savor food and be grateful for the opportunity to do so; to ensure a healthy lifestyle which in turn enables you to accomplish your dreams. It's not just a diet but a unique lifestyle that provokes introspection by altering the food chain.

They say, *'One cannot think well, love well, sleep well, if one has not dined well'*, and if you believe in that, then following this diet becomes an act of loving yourself. If you're flustered with advertisements about diet-pills and in search of something backed by scientific knowledge and research, then the Mediterranean diet should be your go-to choice.

Even if you're a little superstitious, you'd be pleased to know that the horoscope recommends the Mediterranean diet for those who desire rapid-fire results. So, whether you're someone who's looking to shed some pounds or someone who's looking for a 360-degree lifestyle shift, or someone who's just concerned about his health, then I guarantee the Mediterranean diet is the answer to all your problems.

Thank you for reading this book and purchasing, I really appreciate it. If you have enjoyed it/found it useful then please consider leaving a review on Amazon. I am very excited and looking forward to reading each review!

ABOUT THE AUTHOR

Jasmin Walters, an inspiring lady with a PhD in Medical Nutrition & Therapy, based in the USA.

Jasmin leads in her field with nutritional health, dietary advice, natural remedies, healing techniques and alternative medicines. Jasmin's ability to advocate in natural health, therapies, remedies, dietary balances and healing has been producing for more than two decades.

Jasmin has spent more than twenty years researching natural approaches to health, healthy living and healing.

Jasmin shares her knowledge, experiences & research to the rest of the world by guiding people how to live healthier lifestyles.

Jasmin in her journeys has also been an enthusiast of delicious food with homemade recipes. Some of Jasmin's favorite styles are Plant Based Vegan, Mediterranean, Paleo and many more.

Jasmin's love for cooking healthy also stemmed from her childhood, her mom whom she is so thankful to.

Jasmin's inspiration for writing came from her experiences from childhood and developed a keen interest from her father's study of Nutrition in Humans.

If you want to reach out and find out what else I am writing please visit my Amazon author page. Would love to hear more from you all, follow me also at Amazon Goodreads.

Thank you

Jasmin Walters

Printed in Great Britain
by Amazon

46256528R00046